INSIDE

PLUS! PUZZLES AND STUFF

PAGE >> 02
SO YOU'RE STARTING SECONDARY SCHOOL... >>
These pages contain loads of advice to help you as you take this important step. We explo[re] growing up, facing fear, friendships and a wh[ole] lot more!

PAGE >> 26
BIBLE HELP >>
Seven days of Bible reading notes to get you i[n] the swing of spending time with God – the o[ne] who will never break His promises to you, wi[ll] never leave you and will always help you.

PAGE >> 33
OTHER COOL STUFF TO READ >>
It doesn't stop here! Keep digging deeper into God's Word and living life to the full with Him.

WE WANT TO HEAR FROM YOU!

If you have a story to share about school, or a just want to tell us what you think about this guide, then write to us:

Email: **yps@cwr.org.uk**
Post: **YP's, Waverley Abbey House, Waverley Lane, Farnham, Surrey, GU9 8EP, UK.**

BIG FISH, LITTLE POND

Can you remember when you started your first school? How did it feel? How did you feel about the 'bigger kids' there?

Did you ever wish you were in the higher year groups and getting ready to take on 'big school'? Well, now you are! How are you feeling about it?!

You are now changing from being one of the 'big fish' in a 'little pond' to being a 'little fish' in a 'bigger pond' (unless of course you're six feet tall and look sixteen years old!).

When you've been in a school for a few years, you know the deal. You know who all the teachers are, where you should be and when, and most importantly, what day they serve the chocolate fudge cake in the canteen. But when everything's totally new and you have no idea where 'Computer Lab D' is, you can end up feeling like a fish out of water.

But 'little' isn't a problem. Remember Zacchaeus? Take a look at Luke 19:1–10 if you aren't familiar with his story. He was little – a small man in a big crowd – but he didn't let his size get in the way of his plans. He wanted to see Jesus, and he found a way to do it – by climbing a tree.

EVEN THOUGH YOU MAY FEEL SMALL AGAIN, DON'T WORRY

Soon enough you'll know the school like the back of your hand – and in a year's time there will be a load of other people coming who will feel just like you do now. Wouldn't it be cool to be able to help them next year and make them feel welcome? The time will fly by!

LITTLE FISH, BIG POND

FINISHING WELL

Before we look at the thrills, challenges and opportunities of a new school, it's important to think about how you are going to leave your current school. How will your teachers and classmates remember you? What impression will you leave them with?

It's a pretty old movie now but *Cool Runnings* is well worth a watch. A team of Jamaican athletes form a bobsledding team (yep – some Caribbean islanders take on a snow sport) for the Calgary Winter Olympics. They do surprisingly well, but in their last sled run, they crash halfway through the course.

Their dreams are shattered. But – spoiler alert – they don't stomp off home in a strop. The four teammates pick up their battered bobsled and carry it down the rest of the course and across the finish line (and everyone claps and cries with joy, etc). It's a brilliant moment. They finish the race with their heads held high.

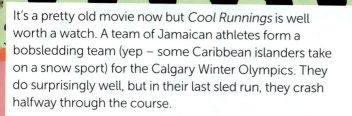

Has school been a bumpy ride for you so far? Maybe you've found your lessons hard or have had a tough time in some of your friendships recently. All the more reasons to finish well! Think about some Bible characters like Jonah, Samson, Peter and others. They all made HUGE mistakes, but with God's help they finished well.

So, even though secondary school is a great chance for a fresh start, do what you can to end this current chapter on a good note. Thank your teachers. Try your best. Make peace with kids that might have bothered you in the past. That's how you finish the race with your head held high.

FINISH THE RACE WITH YOUR HEAD HELD HIGH

LESSONS FROM THE KOI CARP

Ever seen Japanese koi (pronounced 'coy') carp? They are freshwater fish that are often kept as pets. There's something pretty special about koi, and we can learn a lesson from them.

A koi carp will never outgrow its container. For example, if you keep a koi in a small bowl it will only grow to, say, 8cm. Keep it in a bigger bowl and it might reach 15cm. Move it to a pond and it will keep growing to 28cm, but put it in a lake and it will reach a whopping 53cm.

SO... WHAT'S THE LESSON?

In order for us to grow, we often need to be put in bigger 'containers'. Going to a new, bigger school does just that.

Grow how? We're not just talking about growing taller! At your new school, you will learn more and more. Your knowledge of things will grow. Your ability to get on with others and work well together will get stronger. You will be able to solve bigger and more complex problems. You will become more and more mature all round! God wants you to grow. He also wants you to grow closer and closer to Him. With new challenges, we can lean on Him and trust Him to help.

GOD WANTS YOU TO GROW

FACING FEAR

At some point we all find ourselves in a situation that makes us afraid; whether it's in the playground, at home, when we're late with our homework or trying something new for the first time.

Sometimes there is good reason to be afraid, but other times it doesn't make sense. Some people are scared of spiders, birds, small spaces or big spaces – there are even people who are afraid of buttons! Fear doesn't always make sense.

ONE WAY TO THINK OF FEAR IS:

F – FALSE
E – EXPECTATIONS
A – APPEARING
R – REAL

How many times have you been really worried and scared that something would happen… but it never did?

Fear is natural. It's your mind and body telling you to be careful because something might be dangerous or hard. For us as Christians, however, fear is not something that should stop us doing what we know is right.

Jesus is always with us and He'll never leave us. Whatever you're afraid of – whether it's the bigger kids on the bus, or the buttons on your new school uniform – take your fears to God.

Take some time now to think about what you might be fearful of at your new school. Then imagine Jesus with you in these situations.

THE BIBLE SAYS, 'DO NOT BE AFRAID; DO NOT BE DISCOURAGED, FOR THE LORD YOUR GOD WILL BE WITH YOU WHEREVER YOU GO.' (JOSHUA 1:9)

GOD'S FUTURE FOR YOU

THE BIBLE SAYS, "'FOR I KNOW THE PLANS I HAVE FOR YOU,' DECLARES THE LORD, 'PLANS TO PROSPER YOU AND NOT TO HARM YOU, PLANS TO GIVE YOU HOPE AND A FUTURE.'" (JEREMIAH 29:11)

WHAT A FANTASTIC PROMISE!

God has plans for you! Good plans. Plans that will help you grow as a person and as one of His children — just as a tiny acorn grows into a mighty oak tree!

There's often a lot of pressure from our teachers, parents or caregivers as to what we should 'become' later on in life. Maybe people are telling you what they would like you to do for a job; maybe their plan is for you to be a doctor, lawyer, teacher or politician. But for most parents, what they *really* want is for you to be happy and make the most of life. Because they can't see into the future they don't know what will make you happy, and can only give it their best guess. But God is your Father who knows you and the future — He knows exactly what is best for you!

So wherever you go to school and whatever you study there, Jesus will be with you and can help you through it.

THAT DOESN'T MEAN IT WILL BE EASY...

When God promised the Isrealites their own special land, He knew it was going to be a good place for them to settle. He described it as a land of milk and honey — sweet and good. You can read the story in the books of Exodus and Joshua.

If you read the whole story you'll notice something else. Even though the land God promised the Israelites was good, the journey there and actually settling down was anything but easy. In fact, it was very hard. There were battles to fight, their own silly arguments, and other nations poking fun at them and taunting them.

When God promises something He *always* makes sure it happens. But He doesn't always promise that things will be easy or that there'll be no problems. At school, you need to work hard and push yourself to learn. Similarly, God sometimes allows us to be 'pushed' in all sorts of areas of life so that we can grow more like Him. But it doesn't mean He won't come through and give us all that He has promised us.

T'S ATTITUDE THAT COUNTS

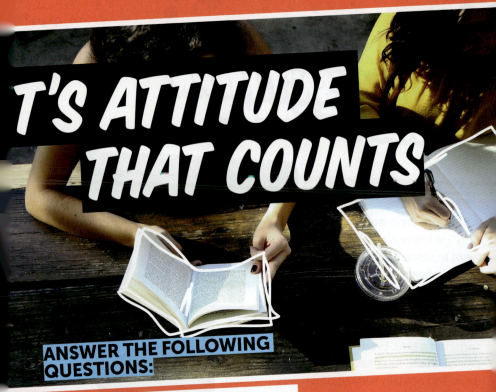

ANSWER THE FOLLOWING QUESTIONS:

ON MY FIRST DAY AT SCHOOL I INTEND TO...
a) avoid lessons and hang around outside.
b) survive, and hope that no one singles me out...
c) be in the right place at the right time.

DURING MY FIRST WEEK OF SCHOOL I HOPE TO...
a) get a detention. That would be hilarious.
b) keep to myself. I'm really shy.
c) make as many friends as I can!

BY THE END OF THE TERM I HOPE THE TEACHERS WILL...
a) want to throw me out of school!
b) not have noticed me.
c) know that I always try my best.

You may have noticed that there are some people at school who don't seem to have to try very hard at anything – they just seem to be able to do everything, and do it well. There are also people who, no matter how hard they try, always seem to find things go wrong for them or they just don't 'get it'. Most of us are somewhere in the middle.

When it comes to school, it doesn't matter where you are on the scale – what matters is your attitude. Doing your best is all you can do, and is all that is expected of you.

THE BIBLE SAYS, 'WHATEVER YOUR HAND FINDS TO DO, DO IT WITH ALL YOUR MIGHT' (ECCLESIASTES 9:10)

SCORES

MOSTLY A'S:
Are you taking this seriously? At this rate, you're going to struggle. Have another think about what you want to get out of your time at school.

MOSTLY B'S:
It seems that you may have some reservations. Ask God for courage and help. He will look after you.

MOSTLY C'S:
Looks like you're gonna be just fine. Remember, it won't always be easy – but a great attitude like yours will really help!

WHERE AM I GOING?!

One of the big challenges when starting a new school is finding out where everything is and making sure you are in the right place at the right time.

HIDDEN BELOW ARE TEN IMPORTANT PLACES YOU MAY NEED TO FIND AT SOME POINT... SEE HOW YOU GET ON!

STAFF ROOM
SCIENCE LAB
BIKE SHED
CLASSROOM

TOILET
GYM
OFFICE

CANTEEN
LIBRARY
MAIN HALL

```
Z G D E H S E K I B W U
M A I N H A L L A P N F
O E C I F F O L X H M I
O H Y E E H E J D S U Q
R K M Y G C A N T E E N
F H T F N M A L L K K K
F T O E J S D L V O F T
A L I B R A R Y H B F R
T C L A S S R O O M O S
S X E S D G B V T P Y F
J A T M L S Q D F D F H
```

ANSWERS ON PAGE 33.

12

URBAN MYTHS

THE BIBLE SAYS, 'KNOW THE TRUTH, AND THE TRUTH WILL SET YOU FREE.' (JOHN 8:32)

An 'urban myth' is a story that most people believe, but is not actually true. Most schools have their own urban myths, like there's a boy in Year 11 who flushes every new kid's head down the toilet, or there's a teacher whose detentions involve jam and bees.

People will believe almost anything, and urban myths even crop up in the Bible. When Joshua was getting ready to go into the Promised Land, the children of Israel had heard there were giants there – huge and terrifying giants! Because the Israelites were expecting to see these giants, they sent a report back saying they felt like grasshoppers and were afraid. This rumour spread through the whole camp until no one was prepared to enter the land.

At school, you may hear many stories that make you feel small and scared. But the truth is that school is full of people just like you, and the teachers are people just like your mum or dad or other adults in your life. Be careful what you believe. God says you are special and precious – and that's no myth.

DON'T FORGET, YOU COULD TALK TO AN ADULT ABOUT THESE KINDS OF STORIES TO CHECK OUT HOW REALISTIC THEY MIGHT BE.

DEALING WITH DISAPPOINTMENT

You may have many hopes and dreams for your time at your new school. But in life, sometimes things don't turn out exactly as we would hope.

DON'T BE DISAPPOINTED IF…

- You are in a different tutor group or house to your friends
- Other pupils get to be with their friends
- You don't make the school sports teams straightaway
- There is someone else better than you at something you were the best at in your old school
- Your teacher seems less fun than others

Unfortunately, disappointment is a part of life and hits us all. The important thing is how you deal with it. Every disappointment in life is an opportunity.

When Jesus died on the cross, the disciples were very sad and very disappointed. Not only was He their friend, He was meant to be their Saviour — and now He was gone. But we know what happened next. He came back to life! Meaning we could have new life too. When disappointment comes, we just need to give it over to God and trust that something even better is around the corner.

MAKING PARENTS' EVENING WORK

Parents' Evening: when those who look after you at home get to meet your teachers face to face to discuss how you are doing. We can find it a walk in the park – or downright scary and unpleasant.

The secret to making Parents' Evening a positive experience is talking to your parents or guardians throughout the year, not just when they get your report. They want you to do well – they won't expect perfection, just that you do your best.

Sometimes it may feel easier to not bother talking to your parents. You may even think they don't understand what school is like. But they've done it all before, and probably remember what their school days were like. Your parents want the best for you. They want you to be happy, so they're interested in how you're getting on.

One simple way to honour them is by speaking with them, being honest with them and allowing them to help when they can.

THE BIBLE SAYS, 'HONOUR YOUR FATHER AND MOTHER' (EPHESIANS 6:2)

HISTORY LESSONS

Changing school is a very normal process and everyone goes through it, but it's OK to admit that it can feel like a pretty big deal!

It can be helpful to choose a few people who you can talk to about things. Think about it — every grown-up has been through it before. Sure, they aren't you and they may not have gone to the school you're going to, but you'll probably find they learned a few lessons along the way that might help you.

Q & As

FIND THREE OLDER PEOPLE AND ASK THEM THE FIVE QUESTIONS ON THE OPPOSITE PAGE. YOU COULD ASK:
- a sibling or cousin
- a leader or member of your youth group
- a leader or member of your church.

OK, so these people can't go into school with you, but remember who can — the Holy Spirit! He is always there with us, knowing how we feel and ready to help.

THE BIBLE SAYS, 'CAST ALL YOUR ANXIETY ON HIM BECAUSE HE CARES FOR YOU.' (1 PETER 5:7)

1. What did you like most at school?
- ....
- ....
- ....

2. What did you dislike most?
- ....
- ....
- ....

3. What helped you deal with what you didn't like?
- ....
- ....
- ....

4. What would be the best advice you could give me?
- ....
- ....
- ....

5. What would you do differently if you went through changing schools again?
- ....
- ....
- ....

JOIN THE CLUB

Let's face it: your new school probably means more homework, more exams, more coursework, more demands… but fear not!

With the more challenging schoolwork that you're going to have, it's a good idea to make sure you have lots of ways to enjoy yourself! Sure, you could just go home at the end of the day and veg out in front of the TV, but sometimes these things don't actually help you to relax.

When you work hard, you need to have some ways to blow off steam, and one of the best ways to do so is by doing something phsyical. For example, you could join some sports, dance or music clubs.

Joining one or two clubs can really help your start at school go well. Clubs help you meet new people and make new friends, and give you new hobbies, interests and experiences.

THERE'S AN OLD SAYING: 'WORK HARD, PLAY HARD'

If your school has a Christian Union (CU) or something similar, join as soon as you can! Having friends at school who are also Christians can be so encouraging. You won't be the only one!

Inviting Jesus into your school life will transform your experience. Something as simple as one lunchtime a week with your 'CU' could make a huge difference. Give it a try, and see what God does!

And if there isn't a CU at your school, why not be brave and start one yourself?

THE BIBLE SAYS, 'LET US CONSIDER HOW WE MAY SPUR ONE ANOTHER ON TOWARDS LOVE AND GOOD DEEDS, NOT GIVING UP MEETING TOGETHER' (HEBREWS 10:24–25)

FRIENDSHIPS

Friends! We all need good ones, especially at school. Some might be coming with you to your new school, but there might be others that you'll be saying goodbye to – for now, at least.

Goodbyes are a natural part of life – friends do come and go. Very few friends remain your 'best friends' for life – it's just impossible to stay in touch with everyone, but that's OK.

Moving on to a new school is a chance to move on from some friendships that you know in your heart aren't good for you and don't honour God. Some people just bring out the worst and not the best in each other.

But it's also a chance to make some new, fresh friendships that will be good for you! There is an old saying: 'Never judge a book by its cover.' This is worth remembering. It's all too easy to look at someone and instantly decide what you think of them, never actually giving them a chance to show you who they really are.

In the Bible, God told Samuel to go to the house of a man called Jesse to choose one of his sons to be king of Israel. Samuel looked at the oldest brother and thought it must be him. But God said, 'The Lord does not look at the things people look at. People look at the outward appearance, but the Lord looks at the heart' (1 Samuel 16:7). Have a look at the whole story to find out what happened.

THE BIBLE SAYS, 'PEOPLE LOOK AT THE OUTWARD APPEARANCE, BUT THE Lord LOOKS AT THE HEART.' (1 SAMUEL 16:7)

CHOOSE CAREFULLY

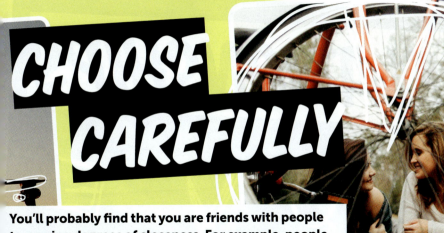

You'll probably find that you are friends with people to varying degrees of closeness. For example, people you'll happily sit and have lunch with might not be the same as your closest friends who you really connect with and tell everything to. Make sure you can trust your closest friends, and that you are a trustworthy friend, too!

It's natural to be nervous on your first day at 'big school'. It's not something you have to deal with every day! But the most important thing is to be yourself, and choose your friends wisely.

When people are nervous they tend to stick to what is familiar or easy instead of holding out and seeing what new opportunities there might be. We talked earlier about taking the opportunity to move on from 'unhelpful' friends, so now it's time to think about what sort of new friends you want to make.

PUT THE FOLLOWING IN ORDER OF IMPORTANCE, FROM 1 (VERY IMPORTANT) TO 5 (NOT PARTICULARLY IMPORTANT).

A NEW FRIEND NEEDS TO…

- [ ] Be cool
- [ ] Be popular
- [ ] Be kind
- [ ] Be genuine
- [ ] Be the same as me

God sees your heart and the hearts of everyone at your school. We all want to be liked, but you will want people to judge you by who you are and not what you look like, so it's important you do the same for others. It's important to give people time to show you who they really are before deciding whether they are going to be close friends.

RELATIONSHIPS

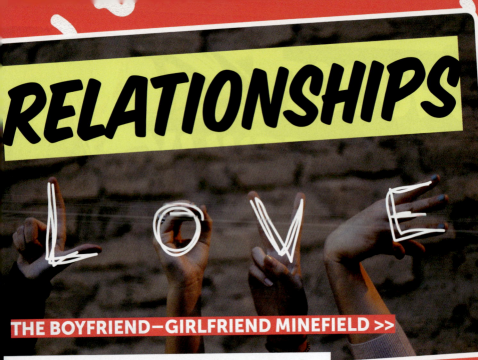

THE BOYFRIEND—GIRLFRIEND MINEFIELD >>

Let's be blunt for a second. That 'big pond' you're now a little fish in is more like a sea of raging hormones. There's a lot of growing up ahead of you, and it's a wild ride!

Secondary school often means that guys and gals start getting a lot more interested in each other, and that's totally OK. But with this can come a lot of pressure, and it can be difficult to not get caught up in the drama of high school romances.

First it's worth saying that, if you enjoy being friends with members of the opposite sex and you're not really interested in dating yet, then do just that! Don't let peer pressure push you into anything. But if you do decide to go out with someone, and your parents don't mind, make sure you think about and really take seriously what God has to teach us about love and relationships. Ask your youth leader, family member or friend at church to discuss this with you. And remember, if that person you're interested is not a Christian — if you can't talk to them about your faith — that relationship probably doesn't have much of a future, so involve God in your decision making.

SCHOOL IS A PLACE OF WORSHIP

THAT MIGHT SOUND A BIT WEIRD, BUT IT'S TRUE

Did you know that you can bring glory to God in anything? You see, when people know that you behave a certain way because of what you believe, that brings God glory — that's WORSHIP.

HERE ARE SOME IDEAS OF WAYS YOU CAN WORSHIP GOD AT SCHOOL:

- Don't bad-mouth your friends
- Help the unpopular people
- Show respect to your teachers

SEE IF YOU CAN THINK OF ANY MORE:

- ....
- ....
- ....
- ....
- ....

LIKE CLOCKWORK

If you read Genesis chapter 1 in your Bible you will notice that God created the world to have 'order'. Think about nature, time, seasons, the human body, your pattern of eating and sleeping — everything has order.

Human beings thrive when things are ordered and running like clockwork. That's why you have a timetable at school, a homework diary and bells for lesson changes.

One of the keys to success in anything is forming a good routine. It's the best way of balancing our work, rest and play — and food and sleep, of course! And in our routine, we can make time every day to spend some moments with God — it's so important!

Think for a moment that time is like money. Adults have to budget their money so that they know they can afford all they buy, along with all the bills they have to pay. When budgeting, they first have to think of the essentials: 'OK, so I need to make sure I have enough money for food and household bills... sorted... now I have this much money left to spend on things I want but don't necessarily need...'

If we were budgeting our time each day, what would be the essentials? Time for school (got to do that), time to eat (yep, got to do that too)... what about time for God? Would you call that essential? Why or why not? If you do think it's essential (and Jesus would say so!) then how can you make this a daily habit?

The good thing with habits is that, once we've made them, they stick and happen quite naturally without us really thinking about it. The hard part is making something a habit in the first place! So first off, we need God's help. Second we need to just get started...

TO HELP YOU MAKE BIBLE READING PART OF YOUR ROUTINE, WE'VE USED THE NEXT FEW PAGES TO GIVE YOU SOME HANDY BIBLE NOTES TO GET YOU STARTED ON YOUR DAILY HABIT! GIVE THEM A GO >>

DAY 01

READ:
MATTHEW 7:24–27

KEY VERSE:
'Therefore everyone who hears these words of mine and puts them into practice is like a wise man who built his house on the rock.' (v24)

You might already know this story well (if you've been to Sunday school you probably know the song and actions!). Sometimes, with well-known stories, we can forget how powerful the meaning is.

GOOD FOUNDATIONS

Jesus explains the meaning behind the story. Anyone who hears and obeys Jesus' teaching is like the man who built his house on rock. The person who ignores Jesus and His teaching is like the man who built his house on sand.

Life is like building a house. Ask yourself, 'Will I build my life on sand or rock?'

Right at the beginning of your school year decide to build your life at school on rock. Jesus is the 'Rock'. Make sure that everything you do is based on Him, and when the storms (problems) come, He'll keep you safe.

THINK ABOUT IT!

How can you lay down good foundations at the start of your new school year?

TALK TO GOD!

Jesus, thank You that You are my rock. Please help me every day to build on You and what You want for my life. Amen.

ACTIONS SPEAK LOUDER THAN WORDS

DAY 02

READ:
MATTHEW 21:28–32

KEY VERSE:
'Which of the two did what his father wanted?' (v31)

In this parable, Jesus reminds us that words don't mean much when actions don't follow them. It's easy to say, 'I'll do my homework after this game,' but if you don't ever get round to it then you'll probably get into trouble.

Why not decide to do few things differently at your new school – like New Year's resolutions?

THINK ABOUT IT!

What is the one thing that you would most like to get right as you start your new school? Why not pray about that now?

TALK TO GOD!

Lord, please give me the courage and help to do what I have said. Amen.

WRITE DOWN THREE OF THOSE THINGS BELOW:

1. ....
....

2. ....
....

3. ....
....

MAKE SURE YOU REMIND YOURSELF OF THEM EVERY DAY UNTIL YOU ARE SETTLED IN AT YOUR SCHOOL

DAY 03

READ:
MATTHEW 16:24–26

KEY VERSE:
'What good will it be for someone to gain the whole world, yet forfeit their soul?' (v26)

THERE'S MORE TO LIFE

THINK ABOUT IT!

Apart from following Jesus, what is the most important thing to you in the world right now?

TALK TO GOD!

Thank You, Lord, that everything I have has come from You. You gave me my body, mind and talents. Please help me to put You first in everything. Amen.

Being a follower of Jesus is the most important part of your life. Yes — it is even more important than school!

Even though being Jesus' disciple is more important than anything else in the world, that doesn't mean other things aren't important at all. But putting God first puts these things into perspective.

Put it this way: you can get everything in the world — the best exam results, job, money, fame and all that goes with it — but if you don't know Jesus it doesn't mean anything. When you die, all those things die with you.

Following Jesus gives meaning to everything else. A great job, money, family and happiness mean something more when you love Jesus. Instead of asking 'What can I get?' you ask, 'What can I give?'

TAKE YOUR BREAD AND FISH

DAY 04

READ:
LUKE 9:10–17

KEY VERSE:
'They all ate and were satisfied' (v17)

The people following Jesus had probably walked a long way, listened to Him teaching for a long time and most had not brought food to eat. Only one boy had a couple of small fish and a few small loaves of bread – that wasn't going to go very far. But Jesus can take whatever we give Him (no matter how small) and He can work miracles with it!

The boy gave what he had to help Jesus. What is it that you can give Jesus at school? Talents? Time? Kindness? It doesn't matter how small you think your gift is, because when we give Jesus something He takes it and multiplies it.

There will be other pupils at school who will be touched and amazed by Jesus if you allow Him to take what you have and multiply it.

THINK ABOUT IT!

What do you think could be your greatest contribution to your new school?

TALK TO GOD!

Lord, I want You to take the little I have and use it for Your glory. Please show me what I have to offer and how I can give it to You. Amen.

29

DAY 05

READ:
MARK 12:28–34

KEY VERSE:
'Of all the commandments, which is the most important?' (v28)

THE GREATEST

LOVE YOUR NEIGHBOUR AS YOURSELF

Jesus was a revolutionary in every sense. His words and actions were often seen as 'different' compared to the normal thinking of the day. The religious leaders thought they understood everything God had said in the past, but Jesus often uncovered new meanings. This caused those who thought they 'knew it all' to become confused, jealous and even angry.

The expert in the law wanted to test Jesus to see if He was a whacky teacher. He asked, 'Of all the commandments, which is the most important?' So, Jesus answered by quoting the teaching of Moses.

The Jews had one main command: 'Love God with everything you've got.' But Jesus expanded this. He added, 'Love your neighbour as yourself.'

You see, Jesus knew the experts in the law ('Pharisees', as they were known) had a habit of saying they loved God with all they had, but they were mean and horrible to everyone else. As far as Jesus is concerned, loving God and loving people go together.

THINK ABOUT IT!

Does your love for other people line up with your love for God?

TALK TO GOD!

Lord, help me to love You with everything I have, and also to love my school friends as well as those I don't get on with. Amen.

GOOD NEIGHBOURS

DAY 06

READ:
LUKE 10:29–37

KEY VERSE:
'Jesus told him, "Go and do likewise."' (v37)

In our previous Bible study we read about the conversation Jesus had with a religious expert in the law. In the reading today another expert (or perhaps the same one) is trying to catch Jesus out by asking more awkward questions: 'So, who's my neighbour?'

Jesus tells the well-known story of the Good Samaritan (it wasn't well known when He told it – He made it up!). The man in the story liked certain people, but couldn't stand Samaritans. Jesus showed that the people we expect to treat us well can be a complete let-down, and those we can't stand surprise us and go out of their way to help.

THINK ABOUT IT!

How willing are you to help other people? Would you stand up for someone you're not friends with if they needed help?

TALK TO GOD!

Lord, help me be a 'Good Samaritan'. Amen.

LET ME HELP YOU

FRUIT

DAY 07

READ:
LUKE 6:43–45

KEY VERSE:
'No good tree bears bad fruit, nor does a bad tree bear good fruit.' (v43)

It's pretty straightforward, really: good trees produce good fruit. Rubbish trees do not produce good fruit. Simple as.

Good people produce good things from their good hearts.

The apostle Paul said, 'I don't do the things I want to do, and end up doing the things I don't want to do.' Do you feel like that sometimes? Now, if Paul struggled with this, then you can be fairly sure most other people will. But Jesus has given us the secret to success. If you want to produce good things then make sure your heart is good.

HOW DO YOU MAKE YOUR HEART GOOD? THE SHORT ANSWER IS…
You can't! But one of the great things about Jesus is that He does for us what we can't do for ourselves. All we have to do is ask and He gives us a new heart. One that's pure and good.

THINK ABOUT IT!
What kind of 'fruit' are you producing right now? What would you like God's help with the most?

TALK TO GOD!
Lord, give me a new heart today; one that will love You and others. Amen.